P9-DCR-809

DISCARD

Red Wing Pottery
with RUMRILL

738.3 SIMON Red

By Dolores Simon

COLLECTOR BOOKS
A Division of Schroeder Publishing Co., Inc.

COVER PIECES

Identification of cover pieces -

Back Row, left to right, Red Wing Pierre French Chef cookie jar, Rum Rill vase, Red Wing stoneware crock.

Front Row, Red Wing dinnerware sign, Red Wing pair Bob White shakers, Orleans teapot, Red Wing stoneware bird feeder, Red Wing wing shape ashtray, Red Wing birchbark canoe planter.

The current values in this book should be used only as a guide. They are not intended to set prices, which vary from one section of the country to another. Auction prices as well as dealer prices vary greatly and are affected by condition as well as demand. Neither the Author nor the Publisher assumes responsibility for any losses that might be incurred as a result of consulting this guide.

Additional copies of this book may be ordered from:

COLLECTOR BOOKS
P.O. Box 3009
Paducah, Kentucky 42001

@$8.95 Add $1.00 for postage and handling.

Copyright: Dolores Simon, Bill Schroeder, 1980
ISBN: 0-89145-116-1

This book or any part thereof may not be reproduced without the written consent of the Author and Publisher.

Printed by IMAGE GRAPHICS, Paducah, Kentucky

Acknowledgements

I would like to take this opportunity to thank the many people who helped me acquire my Red Wing collection. I wish to thank the Goodhue County Historical Society for information given to me. I also wish to express my thanks to the Red Wing Republican Eagle Newspaper of Red Wing, Minnesota. Finally I wish to thank my husband Bob and my children for their effort and assistance. Especially to my daughter Jill, who did all the typing.

Introduction

In 1861, Joseph Pohl, a German immigrant settled on a farm near Red Wing, Minnesota. The town of Red Wing derived its name from an Indian chief and was the home of several early Indian tribes. Using area clay which was found to be excellent in quality, Pohl began making crocks, bowls, and other items and sold them to the local people.

In 1868, David Hallem began producing stoneware in his home in Red Wing. Hallem's business was purchased in 1878 by a group of people who incorporated the Red Wing Stoneware Company. The company trademark was a wing which was ink-stamped on many of the early stoneware pieces. Paper labels and impressed marks were used as early as the 1930's.

In 1883, the Minnesota Stoneware Company was started, giving competition to the Red Wing Company. In 1892, the North Star Stoneware Company opened a plant in the area, causing the Red Wing and Minnesota Stoneware Companies to enter a merger. The new organization was called the Red Wing Union Stoneware Company. The North Star company went out of business around 1896.

In 1920, the Red Wing company began to produce pottery. The early pieces were made with a green stain over a natural tan background. The art pottery line consisted of decoration of cattails, leaves, cranes, etc. Flower pots and vases were manufactured first and were later followed by cookie jars, planters, bowls, jardinieres, and candlestick holders.

By 1936, the name of the company had changed from Red Wing Union Stoneware to Red Wing Potteries Incorporated. Red Wing produced pottery for George Rum Rill of Arkansas during the 1930's. These pieces can be identified by a Rum Rill mark or label. Red Wing kept the contract with this company until it was later given to the Shawnee Pottery Company of Zanesville, Ohio. Red Wing also produced stoneware for the Sleepy Eye Milling Company of Sleepy Eye, Minnesota. By the mid 1940's all stoneware had been completely discontinued by the company.

During the 1930's dinnerware was brought into production at Red Wing. The beginning sales were very promising. The local clay was too crude for manufacturing dinnerware so the company imported clay from several southern states. Dinnerware started out very plain in design and as its popularity increased, many new patterns were added. All dinnerware patterns were hand-painted. Some of these include: Capistrano, 1953; Buffet Royale and Merrileaf, 1960; Daisychain and Random Harvest, 1961; Pompeii, 1962; Lute Song and Pepe, 1963; Damask, 1964; Ardennes, Colonnes, Crazy Rhythmn, Driftwood, Ebb Tide, Fontenac, Golden Viking, Gypsy Trail, Kashmir, Lexington Rose, Lupine, Magnolia (often referred to as Gardenia by collectors), Montmatre, Morning Glory, Mum, Normandy, Northern, Provincial, Quartette, Red Wing Rose, Tampico, Village Brown, Village Green, Water Lily, and Zenia, 1965; Blue Shadows, Bob White, Brocade and Smart Set, 1966. The production dates for dinerware patterns are not definite because several of the more popular lines were in production for more than one year. Bob White is one of the most popular patterns among collectors. The set consists of 42 different pieces plus stands. In 1966, a 45-piece service for eight sold for $59.95. The matching two-gallon water jug with cover and spout is very rare. Trying to boost sales, Red Wing decided to make an improved line of stoneware dinnerware. This was the Cerama Stone, fired at the extremely high temperature of 2200°. It was produced in four patterns--Adobestone, Charstone Bleu, Heatherstone and Greenwichstone. In 1967, the company produced a set of bakeware consisting of bean pots in three sizes, covered casseroles in two sizes, and oval dishes in three sizes.

Red Wing showed a large decline in sales during the 1950's and 60's due to the imports that were flooding the country. As a result, Red Wing Potteries began producing hotel and restaurant china in the early 1960's. They also produced dinnerware for Sears, Roebuck and Company. One popular pattern made for Sears Roebuck was Hearthstone--both in orange and beige. Red Wing dinnerware was used as premium gifts given by the S&H Green Stamp Company and other gift stamp centers.

After a three month labor dispute in 1967, the doors of Red Wing Potteries were permanently closed. The Red Wing factory still stands. It is presently used for storage warehouses. The salesroom is still in operation across the street from the old plant. Single dinnerware pieces are currently being sold, however, complete sets are not available.

Plate I

Row 1

1. Vase, semi-gloss grey, leaf decor, impressed mark Red Wing U.S.A. #1357. 2. Vase, matte green, impressed mark Red Wing U.S.A. #946. 3. Vase, high gloss dark green, stamped mark in circle Red Wing Art pottery. 4. Vase, semi-gloss grey, open scroll handles, impressed mark Red Wing U.S.A. #1351. 5. Vase, matte green, impressed mark Red Wing U.S.A.
Current Value: 1. $7.00; 2. $5.00; 3. $10.00; 4. $5.00; 5. $8.00.

Row 2

1. Vase, high gloss blue with pink interior, impressed mark Red Wing #930. 2. Vase, high gloss burgundy, scalloped open handles, impressed mark Red Wing U.S.A. #1359. 3. Planter Urn, high gloss green, impressed mark Red Wing U.S.A. #871 with gold and red label. 4. Vase, matte white, impressed mark Red Wing U.S.A. #1353.
Current Value: 1. $7.00; 2. $7.00; 3. $8.00; 4. $5.00.

Row 3

1. Vase, high gloss ivory, impressed mark Red Wing U.S.A. #926. 2. Vase, high gloss blue, impressed mark Red Wing and Red Wing Art Pottery label. 3. Vase, semi-gloss brown, impressed mark Red Wing U.S.A. #M-1460. 4. Vase, high gloss grey, dogwood & leaf decor, impressed mark Red Wing U.S.A. #1360.
Current Value: 1. $8.00; 2. $7.00; 3. $8.00; 4. $6.00.

Row 4

1. Vase, matte white, hobnail decor, impressed mark Red Wing U.S.A. #1208. 2. Vase, high gloss green, rose & leaf decor, impressed mark Red Wing Art Pottery #211. 3. Vase, matte brown, swirl decor, gold and red label. 4. Vase, semi-gloss green, leaf decor, impressed mark Red Wing U.S.A. #1174.
Current Value: 1. $6.00; 2. $8.00; 3. $8.00; 4. $7.00.

Plate II

Row 1

1. Vase, semi-gloss white, geese decor, impressed mark Red Wing U.S.A. #M-1456. 2. Vase, matte blue, impressed mark Red Wing U.S.A. #887. 3. Vase, matte white, six-sided, raised mark Red Wing U.S.A. #656. 4. Vase, semi-gloss turquoise, pineapple shaped, impressed mark Red Wing #730.
Current Value: 1. $8.00; 2. $8.00; 3. $8.00; 4. $12.00.

Row 2

1. Vase, matte white, bird & flower decor, impressed mark Red Wing U.S.A. 2. & 3. Pair vases, matte green, ruffled top, impressed mark Red Wing U.S.A. #1203. 4. Vase, semi-gloss orange, eight-sided impressed mark Red Wing U.S.A. #412.
Current Value: 1. $10.00; 2. $6.00; 3. $6.00; 4. $8.00.

Row 3

1. Vase, semi-gloss grey, bulbous with burgundy leaf decor, impressed mark Red Wing U.S.A. #1203. 2. Vase, high gloss chartreuse, square footed with leaf decor, impressed mark Red Wing U.S.A. #B-2003. 3. Vase, semi-gloss blue, leaf decor, impressed mark Red Wing U.S.A. #1155.
Current Value: 1. $8.00; 2. $7.00; 3. $7.00.

Row 4

1. Pitcher, matte green, raised mark Red Wing U.S.A. #M-1565. 2. Vase, matté white, star bursts pattern, raised mark Red Wing U.S.A. #M-1570. 3. Vase, semi-gloss grey, impressed mark Red Wing U.S.A. #404. 4. Vase, matte blue, star studded surface, impressed mark Red Wing U.S.A. #1197.
Current Value: 1. $12.00; 2. $10.00; 3. $7.00; 4. $8.00.

Plate III

Row 1

1. Vase, matte black, raised mark Red Wing U.S.A. #1556. 2. Vase, matte blue, impressed mark Red Wing #899. 3. Vase, matte turquoise, impressed mark Red Wing U.S.A. #886. 4. Planter, matte green, floral decor, impressed mark Red Wing U.S.A. 5. Vase, matte green, floral decal, impressed mark Red Wing U.S.A. #999.
Current Value: 1. $5.00; 2. $5.00; 3. $7.00; 4. $5.00; 5. $5.00.

Row 2

1. Planter, high gloss turquoise speckled, gold handled, impressed mark Red Wing U.S.A. #1210-5½. 2. Vase, high gloss blue, impressed mark Red Wing U.S.A. #951. 3. Vase, high gloss grey, floral decor, impressed mark Red Wing U.S.A. #B-2000. 4. Vase, matte green, impressed mark Red Wing U.S.A. #886.
Current Value: 1. $6.00; 2. $5.00; 3. $6.00; 4. $6.00.

Row 3

1. Vase, matte pink, impressed mark Red Wing U.S.A. #999. 2. Vase, high gloss green, floral decor, impressed mark Red Wing U.S.A. #B-2000. 3. Vase, semi-gloss blue, floral decor, impressed mark on upper handles Red Wing U.S.A. #1161. 4. Planter, matte peach, impressed mark Red Wing #888.
Current Value: 1. $5.00; 2. $8.00; 3. $8.00; 4. $7.00.

Row 4

1. Vase, semi-gloss white, impressed mark Red Wing U.S.A. #1354. 2. Vase, semi-gloss blue, scroll leaf design, impressed mark Red Wing U.S.A. #1105. 3. Vase, semi-gloss grey, burgundy leaf decor, impressed mark Red Wing U.S.A. #1160. 4. Planter, matte green, impressed mark Red Wing #888.
Current Value: 1. $5.00; 2. $7.00; 3. $7.00; 4. $6.00.

Plate IV

Row 1

1. Vase, matte white, shell shaped, impressed mark Red Wing U.S.A. #892. 2. Vase, matte turquoise, small shell shaped, impressed mark Red Wing U.S.A. #897. 3. Vase, matte brown, shell shaped, impressed mark Red Wing U.S.A. #892.
Current Value: 1. $5.00; 2. $5.00; 3. $7.00.

Row 2

1. Vase, high gloss burgundy, cornucopia leaf entwined pattern, impressed mark Red Wing U.S.A. #1097. 2. Vase, high gloss yellow, cornucopia leaf entwined pattern, impressed mark Red Wing U.S.A. #1097. 3. Vase, matte ivory, cornucopia with leaf decor, impressed mark Red Wing U.S.A. #1098.
Current Value: 1. $6.00; 2. $6.00; 3. $8.00.

Row 3

1. & 2. Pair vases, matte ivory, floral and leaf decor, impressed mark Red Wing U.S.A. #413. 3. Vase, matte pink, cornucopia shape, impressed mark Red Wing U.S.A. #1240.
Current Value: 1. $12.00; 2. $12.00; 3. $7.00.

Row 4

1. Vase, high gloss speckled turquoise, cornucopia shape, impressed mark Red Wing U.S.A. #951. 2. Vase, high gloss ivory, cornucopia shape, impressed mark Red Wing U.S.A. #951. 3. Vase, matte blue, shell shaped, impressed mark Red Wing U.S.A. #892.
Current Value: 1. $5.00; 2. $5.00; 3. $6.00.

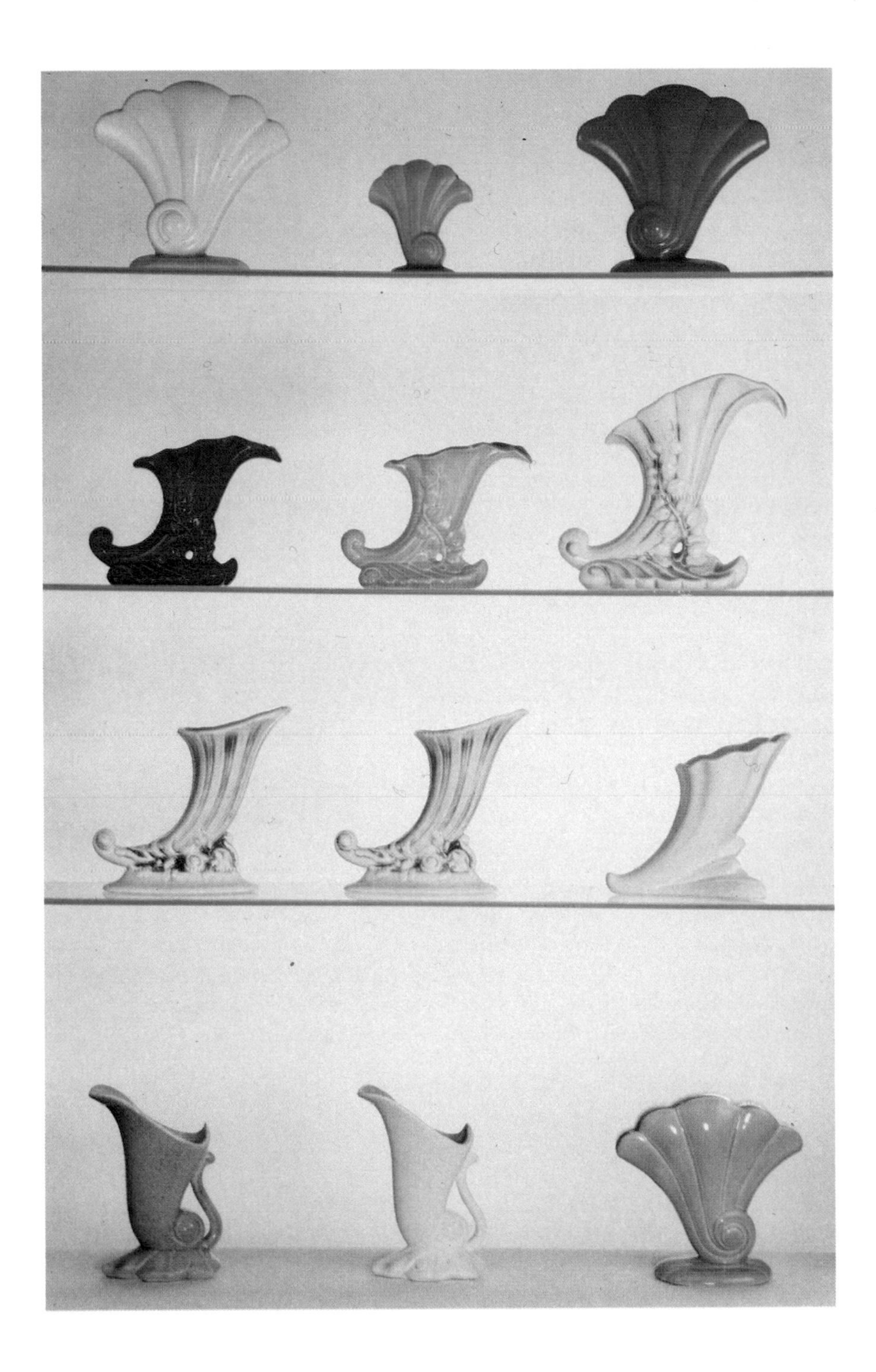

Plate V

Row 1

1. Vase, semi-gloss grey, leaf decor, impressed mark Red Wing U.S.A. #B-1548. 2. Vase, matte pink, raised mark Red Wing U.S.A. #M-5003. 3. Vase, semi-gloss tan and brown, basket weave pattern, impressed mark Red Wing U.S.A. #1137. 4. Vase, matte white, raised mark Red Wing U.S.A. #M-1631.
Current Value: 1. $5.00; 2. $5.00; 3. $8.00; 4. $7.00.

Row 2

1. Planter, matte orange, raised mark Red Wing U.S.A. #790. 2. Planter, matte orange, raised mark Red Wing U.S.A. # 788. 3. Planter, semi-gloss grey, hat shaped, raised mark Red Wing U.S.A. #670.
Current Value: 1. $7.00; 2. $8.00; 3. $8.00.

Row 3

1. Planter, high gloss blue, leaf decor, impressed mark Red Wing U.S.A. #1214. 2. Planter, matte white, pebble surface with orange inner, raised mark Red Wing U.S.A. #884. 3. Vase, semi-gloss white, impressed mark Red Wing U.S.A. #773.
Current Value: 1. $7.00; 2. $7.00; 3. $7.00.

Row 4

1. Vase, semi-gloss copper lustre, sunflower decor, impressed mark Red Wing U.S.A. #B-2002. 2. Vase, high gloss yellow, square shape with cattails decor, impressed mark Red Wing U.S.A. #401. 3. Vase, high gloss rust, bamboo decor, impressed mark Red Wing U.S.A. #1457. 4. Vase, semi-gloss grey, fawn with burgundy leaves, impressed mark Red Wing U.S.A. #1120.
Current Value: 1. $8.00; 2. $6.00; 3. $7.00; 4. $8.00.

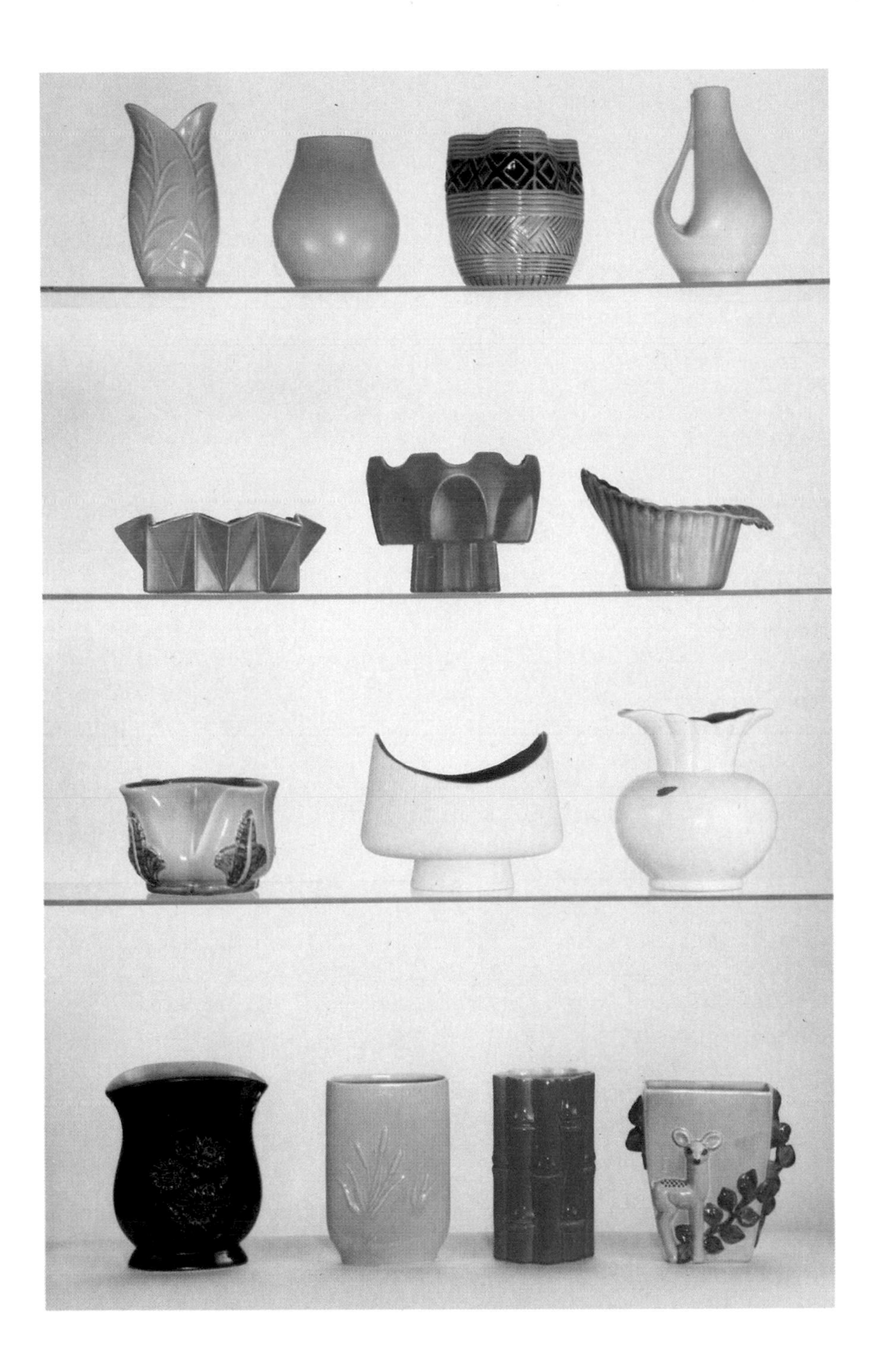

Plate VI

Row 1

1. Vase, semi-gloss turquoise, raised mark Red Wing U.S.A. #795. 2. Vase, high gloss blue, swirl decor, impressed mark Red Wing U.S.A. #952. 3. Hanging planter, semi-gloss pink speckled, has two holes at top for chain, impressed mark Red Wing U.S.A. #M-1598. 4. Hanging planter, semi-gloss green, impressed mark Red Wing U.S.A. #B-1429.
Current Value: 1. $8.00; 2. $6.00; 3. $6.00; 4. $7.00.

Row 2

1. Compote, high gloss turquoise, impressed mark Red Wing U.S.A. #1302. 2. Hanging planter, high gloss brown, impressed mark Red Wing U.S.A. #M-1487. 3. Vase, matte white, impressed mark Red Wing U.S.A. 4. Planter, high gloss pink, raised mark Red Wing U.S.A. # M-1597.
Current Value: 1. $5.00; 2. $7.00; 3. $5.00; 4. $5.00.

Row 3

1. Vase, high gloss grey, tree bark pattern, impressed mark Red Wing U.S.A. #B-2113. 2. Vase, semi-gloss white, fluted decor, raised mark Red Wing U.S.A. #416-10". 3. Vase, semi-gloss rose, fluted decor, raised mark Red Wing U.S.A. #416-9".
Current Value: 1. $6.00; 2. $7.00; 3. $6.00.

Row 4

1. Vase, semi-gloss yellow, fluted decor, raised mark Red Wing U.S.A. #416-10". 2. Lamp, turquoise swirl, impressed mark Red Wing #1025. 3. Lamp, black swirl, impressed mark Red Wing #976. 4. Vase, semi-gloss green, fluted decor, raised mark Red Wing U.S.A. #416-10".
Current Value: 1. $7.00; 2. $18.00; 3. $18.00; 4. $7.00.

Plate VII

Row 1

1. Bowl, matte black, impressed mark Red Wing U.S.A. #M-1493. 2. Planter, semi-gloss lilac, impressed mark Red Wing U.S.A. #B-2016. 3. Planter, matte white, ribbed decor, raised mark Red Wing U.S.A. #1546. 4. Planter, high gloss orange, raised mark Red Wing U.S.A. #665.
Current Value: 1. $5.00; 2. $5.00; 3. $5.00; 4. $6.00.

Row 2

1. Bowl, matte black, raised mark Red Wing U.S.A. 2. Planter, semi-gloss turquoise, footed, impressed mark Red Wing U.S.A. #B-2202. 3. Bowl, matte pink, raised mark Red Wing U.S.A. #M-5006. 4. Planter, matte pink, raised mark Red Wing U.S.A. #M-5032.
Current Value: 1. $5.00; 2. $5.00; 3. $5.00; 4. $5.00.

Row 3

1. Planter, semi-gloss chartreuse, raised floral design, impressed mark Red Wing U.S.A. #B-2011. 2. Planter, high gloss green, impressed mark Red Wing U.S.A. #1463. 3. Planter, high gloss yellow, raised mark Red Wing U.S.A. #M-1572.
Current Value: 1. $7.00; 2. $7.00; 3. $6.00.

Plate VIII

Row 1

1. Planter, semi-gloss blue with pink interior, impressed mark Red Wing U.S.A. #1037. 2. Candy dish, three part hexagon, semi-gloss grey, raised mark Red Wing U.S.A. #801. 3. Tray, matte brown and green interior, impressed mark Red Wing U.S.A. #1037.
Current Value: 1. $5.00; 2. $7.00; 3. $5.00.

Row 2

1. Planter, semi-gloss green with grey interior, impressed mark Red Wing U.S.A. #B-1405. 2. Planter, semi-gloss burgundy with grey interior, impressed mark Red Wing U.S.A. #B-1396. 3. Planter, semi-gloss burgundy with grey interior, scalloped edge, impressed mark Red Wing U.S.A. #1348.
Current Value: 1. $5.00; 2. $5.00; 3. $6.00.

Row 3

1. Planter, semi-gloss turquoise, footed, impressed mark Red Wing U.S.A. #M-1491. 2. Planter, semi-gloss pink speckled, impressed mark Red Wing U.S.A. #M-1447.
Current Value: 1. $5.00; 2. $5.00.

Row 4

1. Planter, matte white, criss cross decor, raised mark Red Wing #637. 2. Planter, matte white, leaf shape, impressed mark Red Wing U.S.A. #1240. 3. Planter, matte burgundy, leaf shape, impressed mark Red Wing U.S.A. #1240.
Current Value: 1. $6.00; 2. $5.00; 3. $5.00.

Row 5

1. Ashtray, high gloss pink, impressed mark Red Wing U.S.A. #695. 2. Planter, matte brown, leaf shape, impressed mark Red Wing U.S.A. #B-1407. 3. Planter, high gloss turquoise speckled, impressed mark Red Wing U.S.A. #1304.
Current Value: 1. $7.00; 2. $5.00; 3. $5.00.

Row 6

1. Planter, high gloss pink, ruffled edge, impressed mark Red Wing U.S.A. #M-1485. 2. Planter, high gloss green, impressed mark Red Wing U.S.A. #1348. 3. Planter, high gloss, tree bark pattern, impressed mark Red Wing U.S.A. #B-2110.
Current Value: 1. $5.00; 2. $6.00; 3. $6.00.

Plate IX

Row 1

1. Planter, matte chartreuse and green interior, leaf shape, impressed mark Red Wing U.S.A. #1387. 2. Planter, matte green, oak leaf shape, impressed mark Red Wing U.S.A. #428. 3. Planter, matte chartreuse and burgundy interior, leaf shape, impressed mark Red Wing U.S.A. #1387.
Current Value: 1. $7.00; 2. $7.00; 3. $7.00.

Row 2

1. Planter, semi-gloss turquoise speckled, leaf shape, impressed mark Red Wing U.S.A. #M-1445. 2. Planter, semi-gloss turquoise speckled, impressed mark Red Wing U.S.A. #M-1446. 3. Planter, semi-gloss grey with chartreuse interior, impressed mark Red Wing U.S.A. #M-1445.
Current Value: 1. $5.00; 2. $5.00; 3. $5.00.

Row 3

1. Planter, semi-gloss brown, impressed mark Red Wing U.S.A. #M-1446. 2. Planter, matte white with green interior, leaf shape, impressed mark Red Wing U.S.A. #1251. 3. Planter, matte green with white interior, impressed mark Red Wing U.S.A. #1251.
Current Value: 1. $5.00; 2. $5.00; 3. $6.00.

Plate X

Row 1

1. Sugar and creamer, matte ivory, grape decor, impressed mark Red Wing U.S.A. #262, #263. 2. Vase, matte ivory art pottery, impressed mark Red Wing U.S.A. #1165. 3. Pair candleholders, matte ivory, grape decor, impressed mark Red Wing U.S.A. #622.
Current Value: 1. $20.00 pr.; 2. $15.00; 3. $20.00 pr.

Row 2

1. Vase, matte ivory, floral decor in relief, impressed mark Red Wing U.S.A. #1190. 2. Plate or liner, matte ivory, grape decor, impressed mark Red Wing #621. 3. Vase, matte ivory, floral decor, impressed mark Red Wing #975.
Current Value: 1. $15.00; 2. $15.00; 3. $10.00.

Row 3

1. Pitcher, matte ivory, double spout, impressed mark Red Wing #766. 2. Bowl, matte ivory, floral rose decor, impressed mark #219. 3. Vase, matte ivory, floral decor, impressed mark Red Wing U.S.A. #1320.
Current Value: 1. $18.00; 2. $18.00; 3. $15.00.

Row 4

1. Wall pocket, matte ivory, gardenia floral decor, impressed mark #1831. 2. Pitcher, matte ivory, gardenia floral decor, impressed mark Red Wing U.S.A. #1219. 3. Wall pocket, matte ivory, gardenia floral decor, impressed #1831.
Current Value: 1. $18.00; 2. $20.00; 3. $18.00.

Plate XI

Row 1

1. Statue, oriental man, matte ivory, impressed mark Red Wing U.S.A. #1309. 2. Planter with deer flower frog, ivory planter art pottery, impressed mark Red Wing U.S.A. #526. 3. Statue oriental goddess, matte ivory, impressed mark Red Wing U.S.A. #1308.
Current Value: 1. $10.00; 2. $20.00; 3. $10.00.

Row 2

1. Planter, semi-gloss turquoise, dachsund puppy, impressed mark Red Wing U.S.A. #1342. 2. Planter with deer flower frog, ivory planter art pottery, impressed mark Red Wing U.S.A. #526. 3. Statue, semi-gloss donkey, impressed mark Red Wing #376.
Current Value: 1. $9.00; 2. $20.00; 3. $9.00.

Row 3

1. Planter, matte black dove, impressed mark Red Wing U.S.A. #M-1467. 2. Ashtray, semi-gloss pink speckled horse, impressed mark Red Wing U.S.A. 3. Cookie jar, semi-gloss green rooster, impressed mark Red Wing U.S.A. #249.
Current Value: 1. $10.00; 2. $10.00; 3. $18.00.

Plate XII

Row 1

1. Planter, semi-gloss green guitar, impressed mark Red Wing U.S.A. #M-1484. 2. Planter, semi-gloss black guitar, impressed mark Red Wing U.S.A. #M-1484.
Current Value: 1. $10.00; 2. $10.00.

Row 2

1. Ashtray, semi-gloss burgundy, figural wing anniversary speciality item 1879-1953. 2. Planter, semi-gloss yellow speckled piano, raised mark Red Wing U.S.A. #M-1525.
Current Value: 1. $15.00; 2. $12.00.

Row 3

1. Vase, matte ivory, birch bark decor, raised mark Red Wing U.S.A. #732. 2. Planter, matte ivory, birch bark canoe, raised mark Red Wing U.S.A. #735. 3. Red Wing advertising sign made for dinnerware, says True China, by Red Wing.
Current Value: 1. $15.00; 2. $20.00; 3. $35.00.

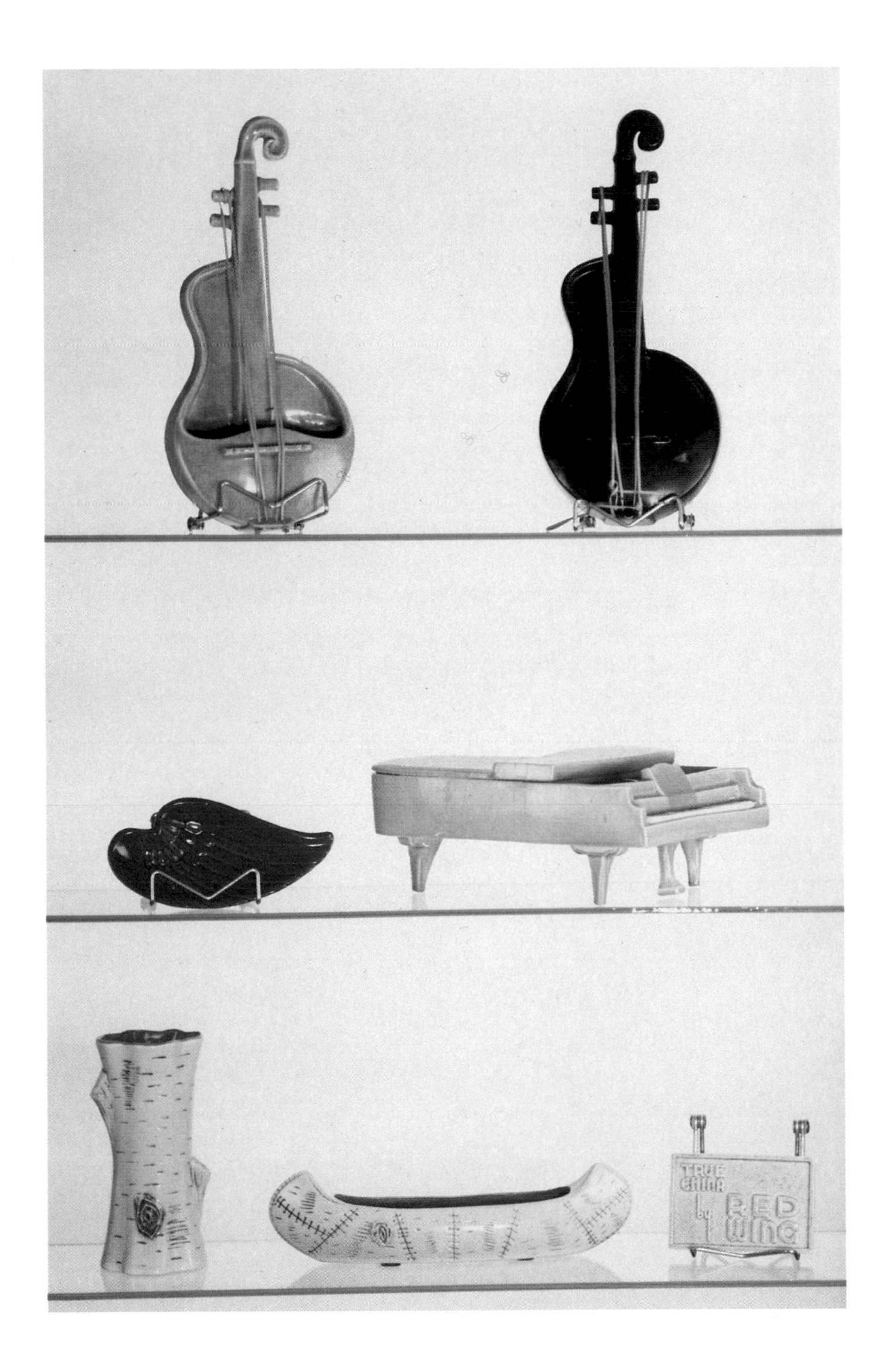
TRUE
CHINA
by
RED
WING

Plate XIII

Row 1

1. Planter, semi-gloss lavender, impressed mark Red Wing U.S.A. #431. 2. Bowl, console, semi-gloss burgundy, impressed mark Red Wing U.S.A. #B-2014. 3. Planter, matte green, raised mark Red Wing U.S.A. #835.
Current Value: 1. $6.00; 2. $8.00; 3. $5.00.

Row 2

1. Ashtray, matte pink, raised mark Red Wing U.S.A. #738. 2. Planter, matte white, square shape, raised mark Red Wing U.S.A. #815. 3. Planter, matte green, raised mark Red Wing U.S.A. #869. 4. Planter, matte green, square, raised mark Red Wing U.S.A. #5018.
Current Value: 1. $5.00; 2. $5.00; 3. $5.00; 4. $5.00.

Row 3

1. Planters, semi-gloss beige, with pink interiors, impressed mark Red Wing U.S.A. #B-1396. 2. Planter, semi-gloss brown, raised mark Red Wing U.S.A. #M-1612. 3. Planter, semi-gloss turquoise with yellow interior, impressed mark Red Wing U.S.A. #1264.
Current Value: 1. $7.00; 2. $8.00; 3. $5.00.

Row 4

1. Planter, semi-gloss grey with pink interior, leaf decor, impressed mark Red Wing U.S.A. #B-1402. 2. Planter, semi-gloss pink speckled, impressed mark Red Wing U.S.A. #M-1477. 3. Planter, semi-gloss brown with green interior, impressed mark Red Wing U.S.A. 4. Planter, high gloss pink speckled, impressed mark Red Wing U.S.A. #1265.
Current Value: 1. $5.00; 2. $5.00; 3. $5.00; 4. $5.00.

Plate XIV

Row 1

1. Candlesticks, pair matte brown, impressed mark Red Wing U.S.A. #B-1409. 2. Candlesticks, pair matte ivory, impressed mark Red Wing U.S.A. #B-1409. 3. Candlesticks, pair matte green, impressed mark Red Wing U.S.A. #B-109.
Current Value: 1. $6.00 pr; 2. $6.00 pr.; 3. $6.00 pr.

Row 2

1. Candlestick, matte white, impressed mark Red Wing U.S.A. #408A. 2. Candlestick, matte grey, impressed mark Red Wing U.S.A. #847. 3. Candlestick, semi-gloss pink, tree bark decor, impressed mark Red Wing U.S.A. #B-2111. 4. Candlestick, matte double turquoise, impressed mark Red Wing U.S.A. #397.
Current Value: 1. $5.00; 2. $5.00; 3. $5.00; 4. $9.00.

Row 3

1. Candlestick, high gloss floral decor, paper label. 2. Candlesticks, pair matte blue, impressed mark Red Wing U.S.A. 3. Candlestick, high gloss burgundy, heart shaped, impressed mark Red Wing U.S.A. #B-1412A. 4. Candlesticks, pair high gloss burgundy, impressed mark Red Wing U.S.A. #B-1411.
Current Value: 1. $6.00; 2. $6.00 pr.; 3. $5.00; 4. $6.00 pr.

Row 4

1. Candlesticks, pair high gloss grey & pink, impressed mark Red Wing U.S.A. #408A. 2. Candlestick, semi-gloss speckled, impressed mark Red Wing U.S.A. #M-4003-8". 3. Candlestick, semi-gloss rose, raised mark Red Wing U.S.A. #1558. 4. Candlesticks, pair matte white & green, heart shaped, impressed mark Red Wing U.S.A. #B-1412A.
Current Value: 1. $6.00 pr.; 2. $6.00; 3. $6.00; 4. $6.00 pr.

Plate XV

Row 1

1. Water jug, matte ivory, impressed mark Rum Rill. 2. Pitcher, semi-gloss chartreuse, impressed mark Red Wing. 3. Water jug, matte yellow, impressed mark Rum Rill.
Current Value: 1. $15.00; 2. $7.00; 3. $15.00.

Row 2

1. Jug, matte blue, wreath & star decor, impressed mark Red Wing U.S.A. #33. 2. Teapot, semi-gloss figural bird, impressed mark Red Wing U.S.A. #207. 3. Teapot, semi-gloss figural bird, impressed mark Red Wing U.S.A. #257.
Current Value: 1. $15.00; 2. $15.00; 3. $15.00.

Row 3

1. Jug, semi-gloss with lid, blue stamped mark Red Wing Art Pottery. 2. Teapot, semi-gloss pink, pumpkin shape, impressed mark Red Wing U.S.A. #235. 3. Teapot, semi-gloss green, pumpkin shape, impressed mark Red Wing U.S.A. #235.
Current Value: 1. $22.00; 2. $15.00; 3. $15.00.

Plate XVI

Row 1

1. Planter, semi-gloss white goose, impressed mark Red Wing U.S.A. #910. 2. Planter, matte white swan, impressed mark Red Wing U.S.A. #259. 3. Planter, semi-gloss white goose, impressed mark Red Wing U.S.A. #910. Current Value: 1. $6.00; 2. $10.00; 3. $6.00.

Row 2

1. Planter, matte blue swan, marked Rum Rill U.S.A. 2. Planters, pair pink flying horses, impressed mark Red Wing U.S.A. #1340. Current Value: 1. $10.00; 2. $12.00 each.

Row 3

1. Planter, burgundy swan, impressed mark Red Wing U.S.A. #259. 2. Planter, matte green swan, impressed mark Red Wing U.S.A. #259. 3. Planter, matte pink swan, impressed mark Red Wing U.S.A. #259. Current Value: 1. $10.00; 2. $10.00; 3. $10.00.

Plate XVII

Row 1

1. Pitcher, matte white, raised mark Red Wing U.S.A. #882. 2. Casserole with lid, semi-gloss stoneware, people & floral decor, no mark. 3. Jar, matte white, raised mark Red Wing U.S.A.
Current Value: 1. $5.00; 2. $20.00; 3. $5.00.

Row 2

1. Toothpick holder, semi-gloss yellow, impressed mark Red Wing U.S.A. 2. Vase, semi-gloss brown, impressed mark Red Wing U.S.A. #1457. 3. Planter, semi-gloss pink, impressed mark Red Wing U.S.A. 4. Vase, matte white floral decor, impressed mark Red Wing U.S.A. #1297. 5. Lamp, miniature matte brown, impressed mark Red Wing U.S.A. #572. 6. Vase, matte grey, raised mark Red Wing U.S.A. #5031. 7. Planter, high gloss blue, impressed mark Red Wing.
Current Value: 1. $4.00; 2. $8.00; 3. $4.00; 4. $8.00; 5. $8.00; 6. $6.00; 7. $5.00.

Row 3

1. Planter, matte white & green, impressed mark Red Wing U.S.A. #278. 2. Ewer, matte pink, impressed mark Red Wing U.S.A. #M-1510. 3. Planter, high gloss grey, impressed mark Red Wing U.S.A. #276. 4. Ewer, high gloss copper lustre, raised mark Red Wing U.S.A. #946. 5. Planter, semi-gloss turquoise, impressed mark Red Wing U.S.A. #278.
Current Value: 1. $6.00; 2. $7.00; 3. $5.00; 4. $10.00; 5. $7.00.

Row 4

1. Cookie jar, stoneware people & floral decor, no mark. 2. Cookie jar, stoneware, stamped mark Red Wing Saffonware. 3. Cookie jar, stoneware, stamped mark Red Wing Art Pottery #21.
Current Value: 1. $20.00; 2. $20.00; 3. $20.00.

Plate XVIII

Row 1

1. Cookie jar, Katrina, ivory, impressed mark Red Wing U.S.A. 2. Cookie jar, Katrina, blue, impressed mark Red Wing U.S.A.
Current Value: 1. $25.00; 2. $25.00.

Row 2

1. Cookie jar, Friar Tuck monk, stamped mark of a wing, hand painted. 2. Cookie jar, Friar Tuck monk, ivory, stamped mark of a wing, hand painted. 3. Cookie jar, Friar Tuck monk, green, stamped mark of a wing, hand painted.
Current Value: 1. $30.00; 2. $30.00; 3. $30.00.

Row 3

1. Cookie jar, French chef Pierre, yellow, stamped wing, marked Red Wing Pottery, hand painted. 2. Cookie jar, Friar Tuck monk, blue, stamped wing, hand painted. 3. Cookie jar, French chef Pierre, ivory, stamped wing marked Red Wing Pottery, hand painted.
Current Value: 1. $27.00; 2. $30.00; 3. $27.00.

Plate XIX

Row 1

1. Bowl, high gloss yellow, pear shape, impressed mark Red Wing U.S.A. 2. Bowl, high gloss pink, pear shape, impressed mark Red Wing U.S.A.
Current Value: 1. $12.00; 2. $12.00.

Row 2

1. Cookie jar, high gloss turquoise, apple shape, impressed mark Red Wing. 2. Jam pot, high gloss green, apple shape, impressed mark Red Wing U.S.A. 3. Cookie jar, semi-gloss turquoise, bunch of bananas, impressed mark Red Wing U.S.A.
Current Value: 1. $22.00; 2. $10.00; 3. $30.00.

Row 3

1. Planter, semi-gloss white, apple shape, impressed mark Red Wing U.S.A. #982. 2. Cookie jar, high gloss pink, pear shape, impressed mark Red Wing U.S.A. 3. Planter, semi-gloss white, pear shape, impressed mark Red Wing U.S.A. #931.
Current Value: 1. $6.00; 2. $25.00; 3. $7.00.

Dinnerware

The dinnerware sets were made in several shapes. The pieces shown in the following book plates are as follows:

Iris	Concord shape
Normandy	Provincial shape
Magnolia	Concord shape
Country Garden	Anniversary shape
Orleans	Provincial shape
Buttercup	Futura shape
Montmarte	Futura shape
Smart Set	Casual shape
Driftwood	Anniversary shape
Northern Lites	Futura shape
Lotus	Concord shape
Lanterns	Concord shape
Grey Spice	Anniversary shape
Green Spice	Anniversary shape
Pink Spice	Anniversary shape
Plum Blossom	Chinese shape
Blossom Time	Concord shape
Zinnia	Concord shape
Morning Glory	Concord shape
Chrysanthemum	Concord shape
Lexington	Concord shape
Capistrano	Anniversary shape
Quartet	Concord shape
Random Harvest	Futura shape
Fruits	Concord shape
Lute Song	Casual shape
Bob White	Casual shape
Two Step	Provincial shape
Brittany	Provincial shape
Pompeii	Casual shape
Tampico	Futura shape

While keeping the shape of the dinner sets the same, the company was able to re-use the same molds for several years.

Plate XX

Row 1

1. Bob White vinegar, oil cruet set with copper stand. 2. Bob White butter dish. 3. Bob White large water pitcher.
Current Value: 1. $35.00; 2. $20.00; 3. $18.00.

Row 2

1. Bob White salad plate. 2. Bob White cereal bowl. 3. Bob White divided vegetable dish.
Current Value: 1. $4.00; 2. $4.00; 3. $12.00.

Row 3

1. Bob White dinner plate. 2. Bob White tall salt & pepper shakers. 3. Bob White handled tidbit. 4. Bob White cup & saucer set.
Current Value: 1. $5.00; 2. $15.00; 3. $17.00; 4. $9.00.

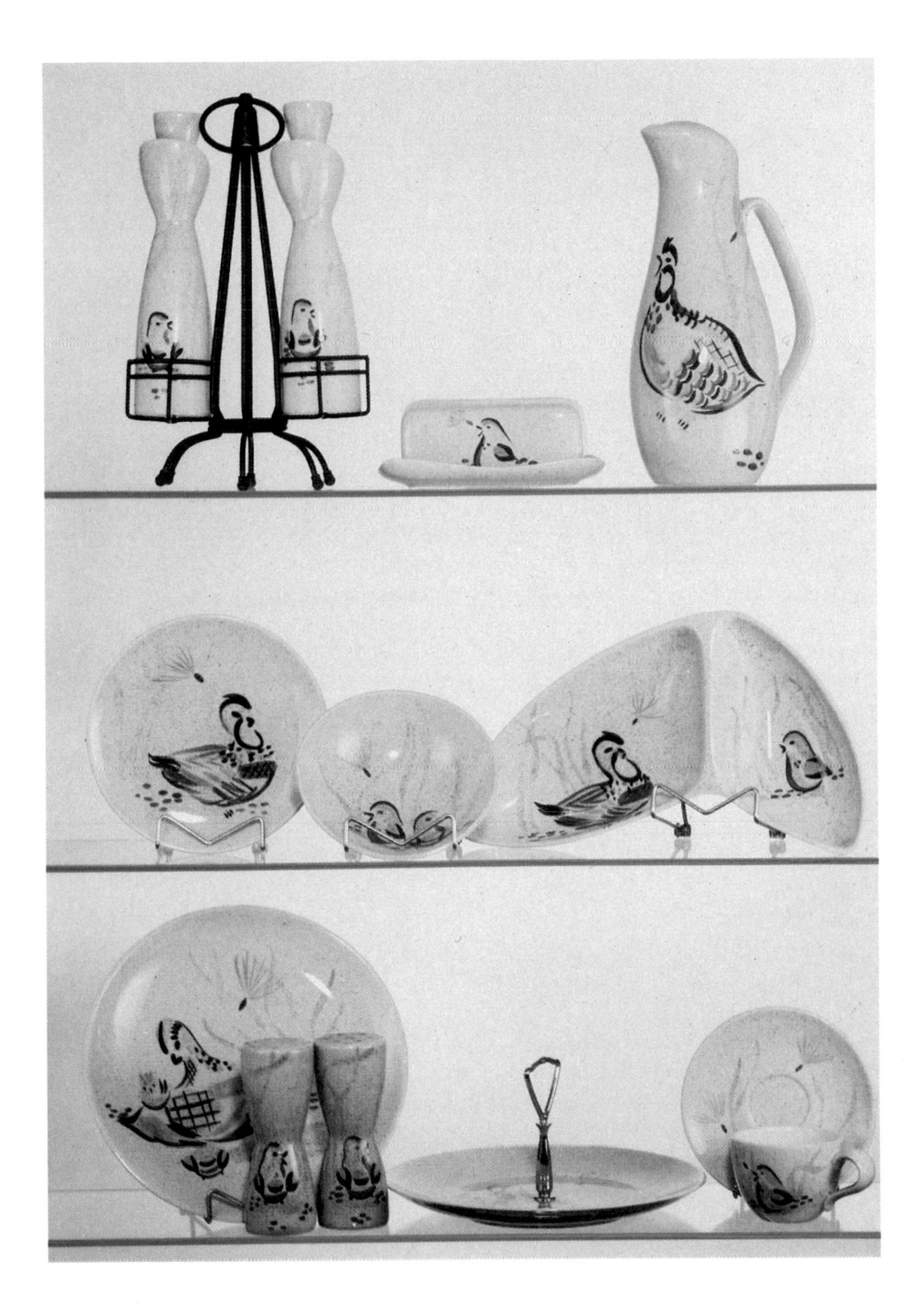

Plate XXI

Row 1

1. Bob White cookie jar, casual shape. 2. Bob White four quart casserole with copper stand.
Current Value: 1. $35.00; 2. $35.00.

Row 2

1. Wrought iron stand for two-piece casserole set.
Current Value: 1. $10.00.

Row 3

1. Bob White covered sugar and creamer on cocktail tray. 2. Bob White Hors d' oeuvre holder and nut bowl. 3. Bob White rim soup. 4. Pair short salt & pepper shakers.
Current Value: 1. $30.00; 2. $35.00; 3. $15.00; 4. $4.50.

Plate XXII

Row 1

1. Tampico casserole. 2. Tampico 8½" plate.
Current Value: 1. $12.00; 2. $4.00.

Row 2

1. Tampico cream pitcher. 2. Tampico 15" platter. 3. Tampico sugar bowl.
Current Value: 1. $6.00; 2. $8.00; 3. $6.00.

Row 3

1. Tampico cup & saucer set. 2. Tampico 10½" plate. 3. Tampico 6½" plate.
Current Value: 1. $8.00; 2. $5.00; 3. $3.00.

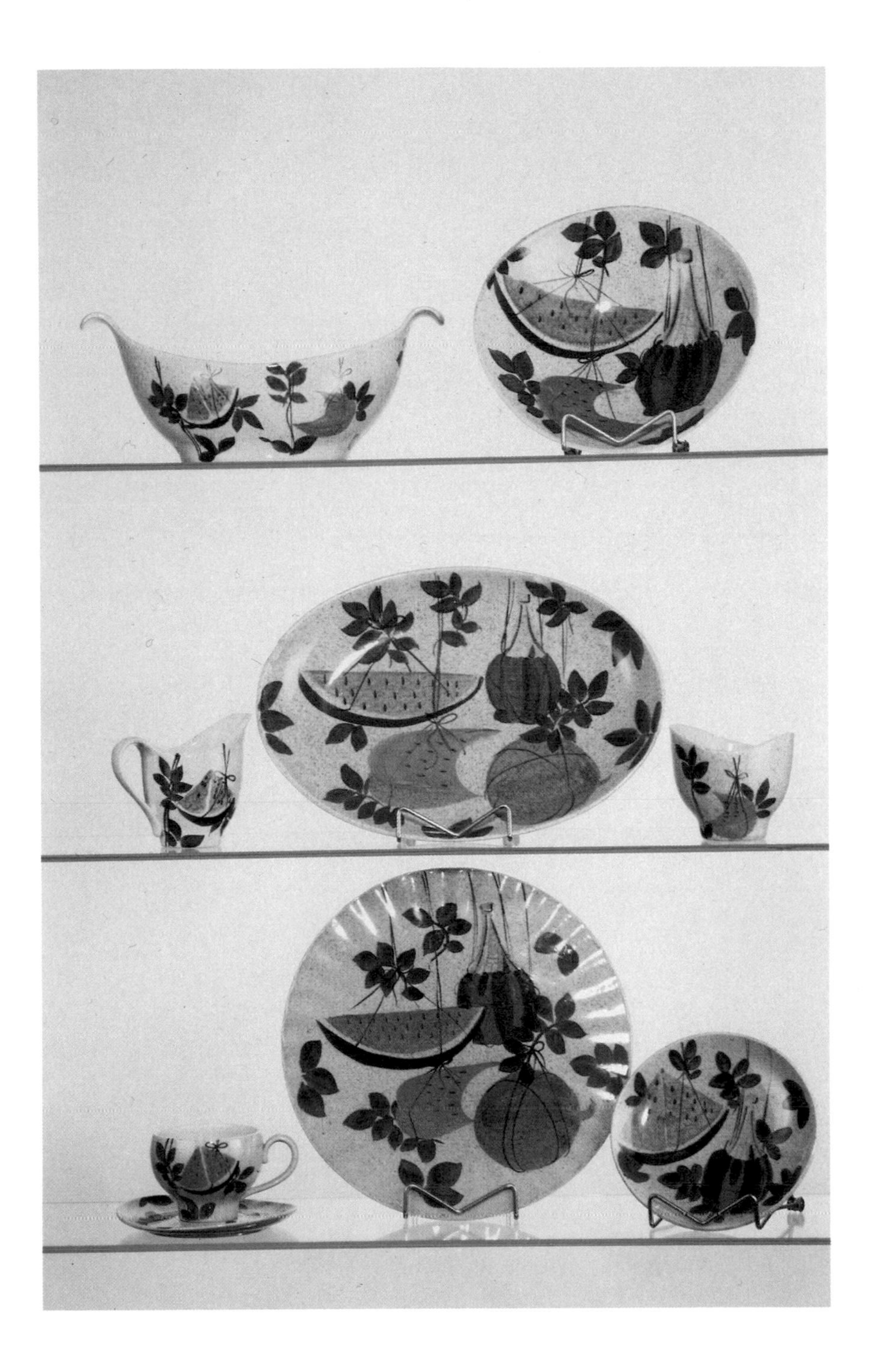

Plate XXIII

Row 1

1. Tampico plate. 2. Tampico teapot. 3. Tampico butter dish.
Current Value: 1. $4.00; 2. $18.00; 3. $15.00.

Row 2

1. Tampico 13" platter.
Current Value: 1. $10.00.

Row 3

1. Tampico plate. 2. Tampico tiered tidbit tray. 3. Tampico cup & saucer set.
Current Value: 1. $4.00; 2. $10.00; 3. $9.00.

Plate XXIV

Row 1

1. Plum Blossom, chinese shape green salt & pepper shakers. 2. Plum Blossom dinner plate. 3. Plum Blossom sugar bowl. 4. Plum Blossom sauce dish.
Current Value: 1. $7.00; 2. $5.00; 3. $6.00; 4. $4.00.

Row 2

1. Plum Blossom green bread plate. 2. Plum Blossom cup & saucer set. 3. Plum Blossom salad plate.
Current Value: 1. $4.00; 2. $6.50; 3. $4.00.

Row 3

1. Plum Blossom cream pitcher. 2. Plum Blossom platter. 3. Plum Blossom covered sugar bowl.
Current Value: 1. $6.00; 2. $7.00; 3. $7.00.

Plate XXV

Row 1

1. Plum Blossom chinese shape pink bread plate. 2. Plum Blossom chinese shape casserole copper lustre. 3. Plum Blossom pink dish.
Current Value: 1. $4.00; 2. $8.00; 3. $8.00.

Row 2

1. Plum Blossom pink luncheon plate. 2. Plum Blossom pink cup & saucer set. 3. Plum Blossom pink demitasse cup & saucer set. 4. Plum Blossom pink dinner plate.
Current Value: 1. $4.50; 2. $8.00; 3. $9.00; 4. $5.00.

Row 3

1. Blossom Time concord shape dinner plate. 2. Blossom Time tray. 3. Front - Blossom Time snack tray. 4. Front - Blossom Time snack tray cup. 5. Blossom Time copper lustre cup.
Current Value: 1. $5.00; 2. $5.00; 3. $5.00; 4. $4.00; 5. $4.00

Plate XXVI

Row 1

1. Blossom Time concord shape plate. 2. Blossom Time dish with cocktail tray. 3. Blossom Time plate. 4. Blossom Time plate. 5. Blossom Time covered onion soup.
Current Value: 1. $4.00; 2. $8.00; 3. $5.00; 4. $5.00; 5. $6.00.

Row 2

1. Pompeii dinner plate. 2. Pompeii cup & saucer set. 3. Pompeii salad plate. 4. Pompeii bowl.
Current Value: 1. $5.00; 2. $9.00; 3. $4.00; 4. $5.00.

Row 3

1. Lute Song casual shape dinner plate. 2. Lute Song cup & saucer set. 3. Normandy dinner plate provincial shape. 4. Normandy cup & saucer set.
Current Value: 1. $5.00; 2. $9.00; 3. $9.00; 4. $6.00.

Plate XXVII

Row 1

1. Lanterns concord shape bread plate. 2. Lanterns salad plate. 3. Lanterns saucer.
Current Value: 1. $4.00; 2. $4.00; 3. $3.00.

Row 2

1. Lanterns row of dinner plates.
Current Value: 1. $5.00 each.

Row 3

1. Lanterns cocktail tray with sauce dish. 2. Lanterns vegetable bowl. 3. Lanterns cocktail tray with sauce dish.
Current Value: 1. $10.00; 2. $8.00; 3. $10.00.

Row 4

1. Lanterns row of cup & saucer sets.
Current Value: 1. $8.00 each set.

Plate XXVIII

Row 1

1. Smart Set casual shape pair tall salt & pepper shakers. 2. Smart Set beverage server and stopper. 3. Smart Set cream pitcher.
Current Value: 1. $12.00; 2. $18.00; 3. $7.00.

Row 2

1. Smart Set sugar with cover. 2. Smart Set cocktail tray. 3. Smart Set handled marmite.
Current Value: 1. $7.00; 2. $6.00; 3. $7.00.

Row 3

1. Smart Set cereal bowl. 2. Smart Set divided vegetable bowl. 3. Smart Set dish.
Current Value: 1. $5.00; 2. $7.00; 3. $5.00.

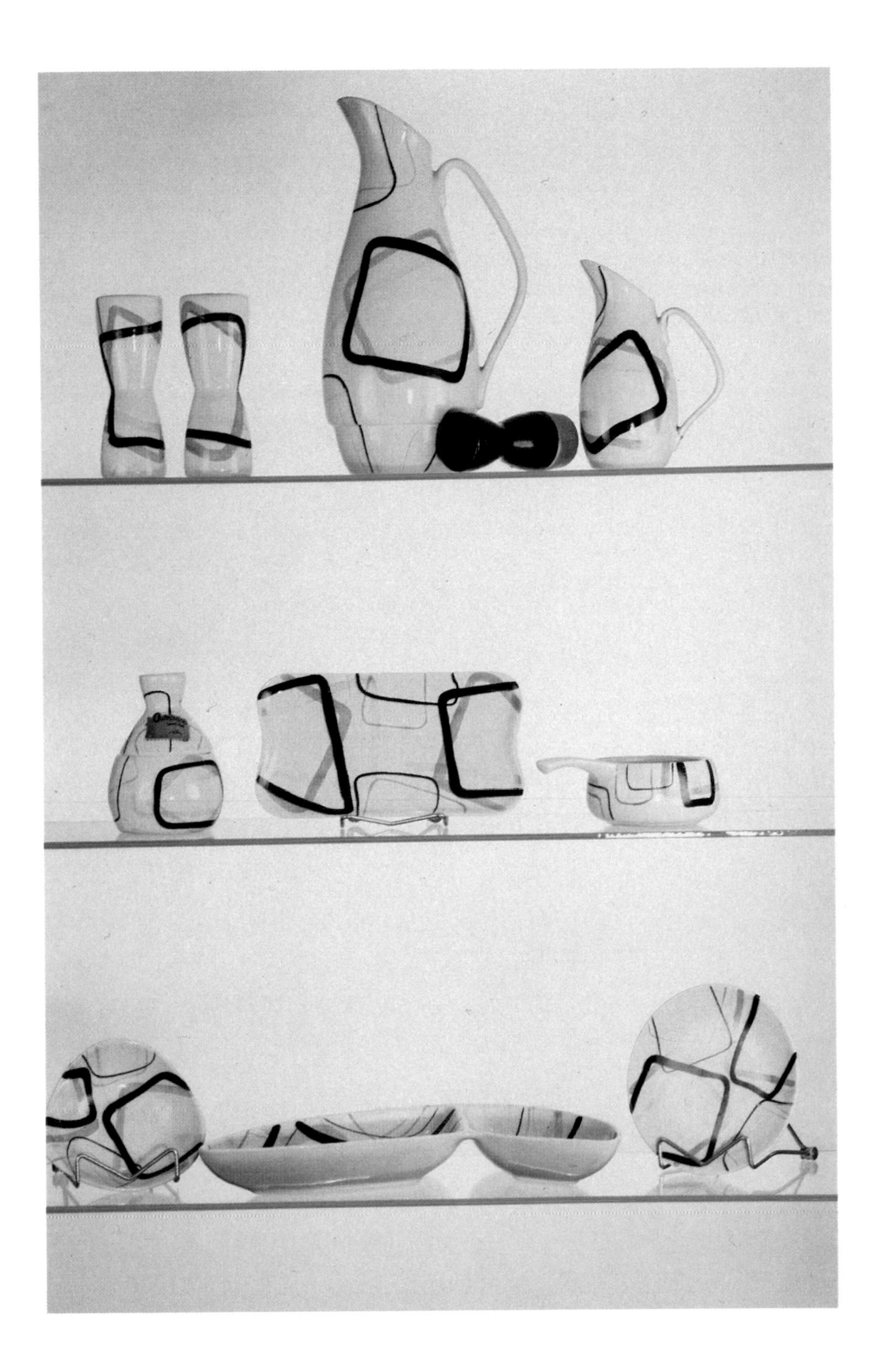

Plate XXIX

Row 1

1. Zinnia concord shape covered onion soup. 2. Zinnia cream pitcher. 3. Zinnia snack tray. 4. Zinnia spoon rest. 5. Zinnia sauce dish.
Current Value: 1. $7.00; 2. $6.00; 3. $5.00; 4. $5.00; 5. $4.00.

Row 2

1. Zinnia dinner plate concord shape. 2. Zinnia gravy boat with attached liner. 3. Zinnia covered butter dish.
Current Value: 1. $5.00; 2. $7.00; 3. $12.00.

Row 3

1. Zinnia three-section dish. 2. Zinnia teapot. 3. Zinnia pair salt & pepper shakers. 4. Zinnia bowl.
Current Value: 1. $7.00; 2. $15.00; 3. $5.00; 4. $6.00.

Plate XXX

Row 1

1. Village Green bread plate. 2. Village Green dinner plate. 3. Village Brown covered marmite.
Current Value: 1. $4.00; 2. $8.00; 3. $5.00.

Row 2

1. Village Green luncheon plate. 2. Village Green platter. 3. Village Green rim soup.
Current Value: 1. $5.00; 2. $7.00; 3. $6.00.

Row 3

1. Village Brown divided vegetable dish. 2. Village Brown covered baking dish.
Current Value: 1. $7.00; 2. $7.00.

Plate XXXI

Row 1

1. Oomph Ware cup & saucer set. 2. Oomph Ware pair salt & pepper shakers. 3. Oomph Ware covered sugar. 4. Oomph Ware creamer. 5. Buttercup covered sugar, futura shape. 6. Buttercup cream pitcher.
Current Value: 1. $8.00; 2. $7.00; 3. $6.00; 4. $6.00; 5. $6.00; 6. $6.00.

Row 2

1. Country Garden anniversary shape bread plate. 2. Country Garden vegetable bowl. 3. Country Garden sauce dish.
Current Value: 1. $5.00; 2. $8.00; 3. $5.00.

Row 3

1. Capistrano anniversary shape vegetable bowl. 2. Capistrano divided vegetable dish. 3. Capistrano 13" platter.
Current Value: 1. $8.00; 2. $10.00; 3. $12.00.

Plate XXXII

Row 1

1. Northern Lites futura shape luncheon plate. 2. Northern Lites salad plate.
Current Value: 1. $4.00; 2. $4.00.

Row 2

1. Northern Lites dinner plate. 2. Northern Lites cup & saucer set. 3. Northern Lites plates.
Current Value: 1. $5.00; 2. $8.00; 3. $5.00.

Row 3

1. Northern Lites cereal dish. 2. Northern Lites plate. 3. Northern Lites cup & saucer set.
Current Value: 1. $5.00; 2. $5.00; 3. $8.00.

Plate XXXIII

Row 1

1. Zinnia pair concord shape yellow shakers. 2. Zinnia 13" platter. 3. Zinnia cup & saucer set.
Current Value: 1. $6.00; 2. $9.00; 3. $8.00.

Row 2

1. Zinnia bread & butter plate. 2. Zinnia dinner plate. 3. Zinnia vegetable bowl.
Current Value: 1. $4.00; 2. $5.00; 3. $7.00.

Row 3

1. Chrysanthemum covered sugar bowl with pink base concord shape. 2. Chrysanthemum purple gravy and liner. 3. Chrysanthemum teapot, purple.
Current Value: 1. $7.00; 2. $8.00; 3. $12.00.

Plate XXXIV

Row 1

1. Iris bread & butter plate, concord shape. 2. Iris large water pitcher, purple. 3. Iris saucer concord shape.
Current Value: 1. $4.00; 2. $12.00; 3. $4.00.

Row 2

1. Iris divided relish dish. 2. Iris pair shakers, purple. 3. Iris gravy boat. 4. Iris 13" platter.
Current Value: 1. $7.00; 2. $7.00; 3. $10.00; 4. $10.00.

Row 3

1. Iris vegetable bowl, concord shape. 2. Iris spoon rest. 3. Iris covered French casserole.
Current Value: 1. $7.00; 2. $7.00; 3. $15.00.

Plate XXXV

Row 1

1. Iris covered sugar. 2. Iris teapot. 3. Iris onion soup. 4. Iris spoon rest. 5. Iris cup & saucer set.
Current Value: 1. $7.00; 2. $15.00; 3. $10.00; 4. $5.00; 5. $8.00.

Row 2

1. Fruits rim soup, concord shape. 2. Fruits three section relish. 3. Fruits pair shakers. 4. Iris gravy boat with liner. 5. Iris cream pitcher.
Current Value: 1. $6.00; 2. $8.00; 3. $7.00; 4. $8.00; 5. $7.00.

Row 3

1. Fruits vegetable bowl. 2. Fruits snack plate & cup. 3. Fruits butter dish. 4. Fruits vegetable bowl.
Current Value: 1. $8.00; 2. $9.00; 3. $12.00; 4. $8.00.

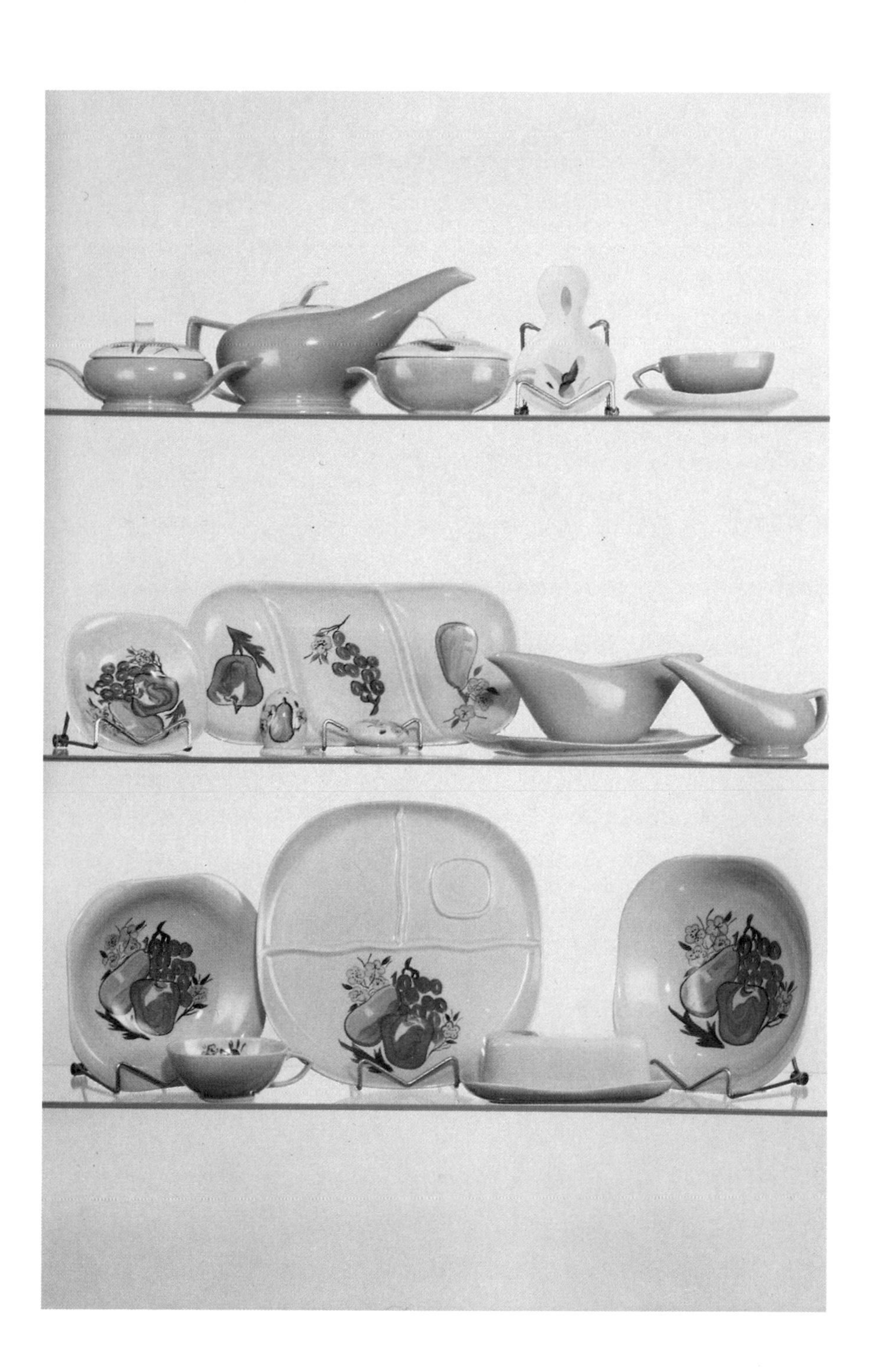

Plate XXXVI

Row 1

1. Magnolia teapot, grey base. 2. Magnolia gravy boat, grey. 3. Magnolia large water pitcher, grey.
Current Value: 1. $15.00; 2. $8.00; 3. $12.00.

Row 2

1. Magnolia tray. 2. Magnolia dinner plate. 3. Magnolia divided relish dish, concord shape.
Current Value: 1. $7.00; 2. $5.00; 3. $7.00.

Row 3

1. Magnolia covered sugar bowl. 2. Magnolia spoon rest. 3. Magnolia shakers concord shape. 4. Magnolia vegetable dish, divided. 5. Magnolia butter dish with grey base.
Current Value: 1. $7.00; 2. $5.00; 3. $6.00; 4. $7.00; 5. $10.00.

Plate XXXVII

Row 1

1. Quartet copper glow divided vegetable dish. 2. Quartet copper glow butter dish. 3. Quartet copper glow tray.
Current Value: 1. $8.00; 2. $10.00; 3. $7.00.

Row 2

1. Mulberry vegetable dish. 2. Quartet copper glow vegetable dish. 3. Mulberry divided vegetable dish.
Current Value: 1. $8.00; 2. $8.00; 3. $9.00.

Row 3

1. Mulberry dessert dish. 2. Mulberry butter dish. 3. Mulberry dinner plate. 4. Mulberry cup & saucer set.
Current Value: 1. $5.00; 2. $10.00; 3. $5.00; 4. $8.00.

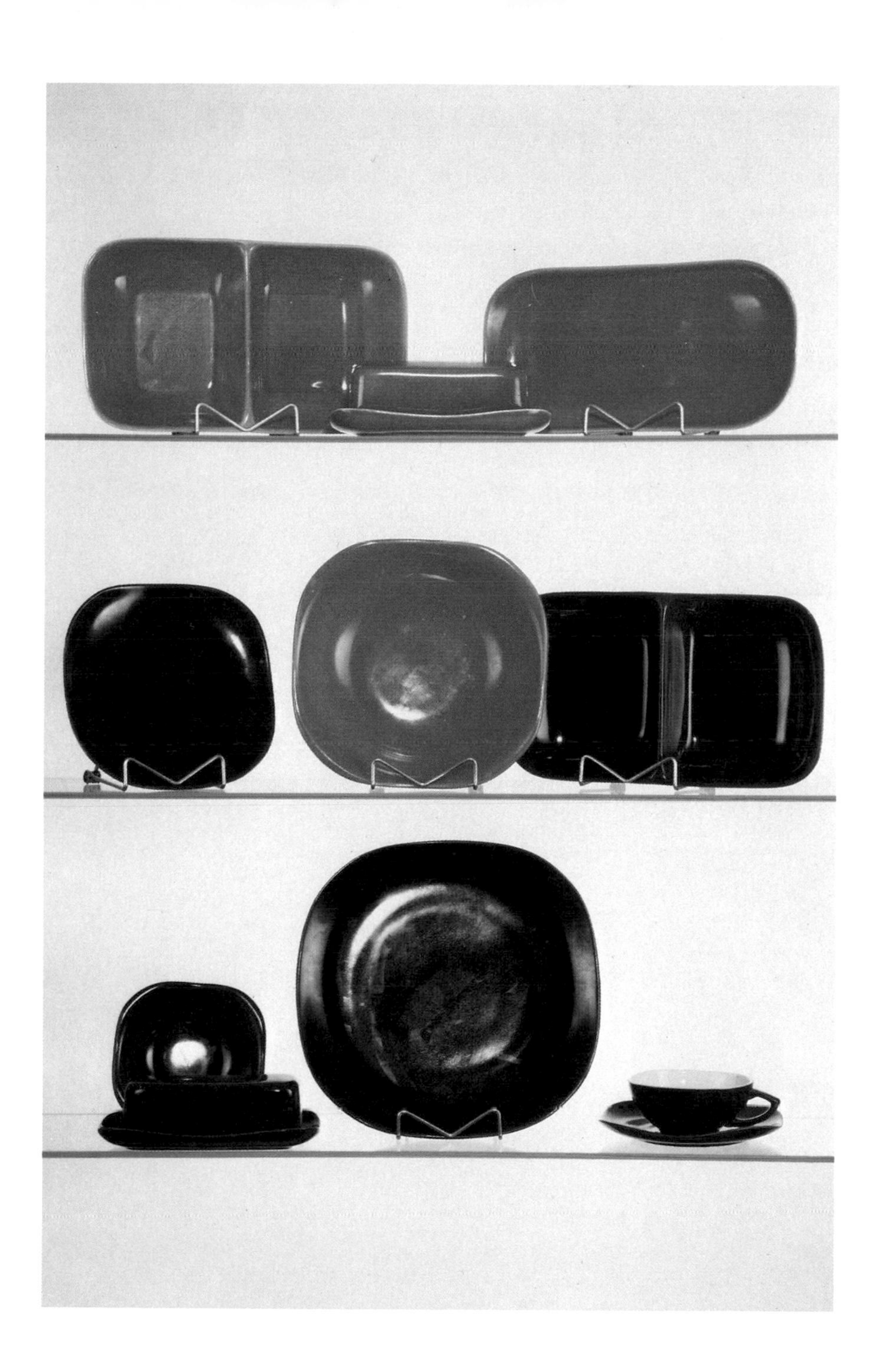

Plate XXXVIII

Row 1

1. Quartet ming green water pitcher. 2. Quartet chartreuse butter dish. 3. Quartet ming green coffee pot.
Current Value: 1. $15.00; 2. $12.00; 3. $15.00.

Row 2

1. Quartet ming green, divided vegetable dish. 2. Quartet ming green vegetable dish. 3. Quartet ming green tray.
Current Value: 1. $8.00; 2. $8.00; 3. $5.00.

Row 3

1. Quartet chartreuse tray. 2. Quartet ming green butter dish. 3. Quartet ming green covered sugar bowl. 4. Quartet chartreuse divided vegetable dish.
Current Value: 1. $5.00; 2. $12.00; 3. $6.00; 4. $8.00.

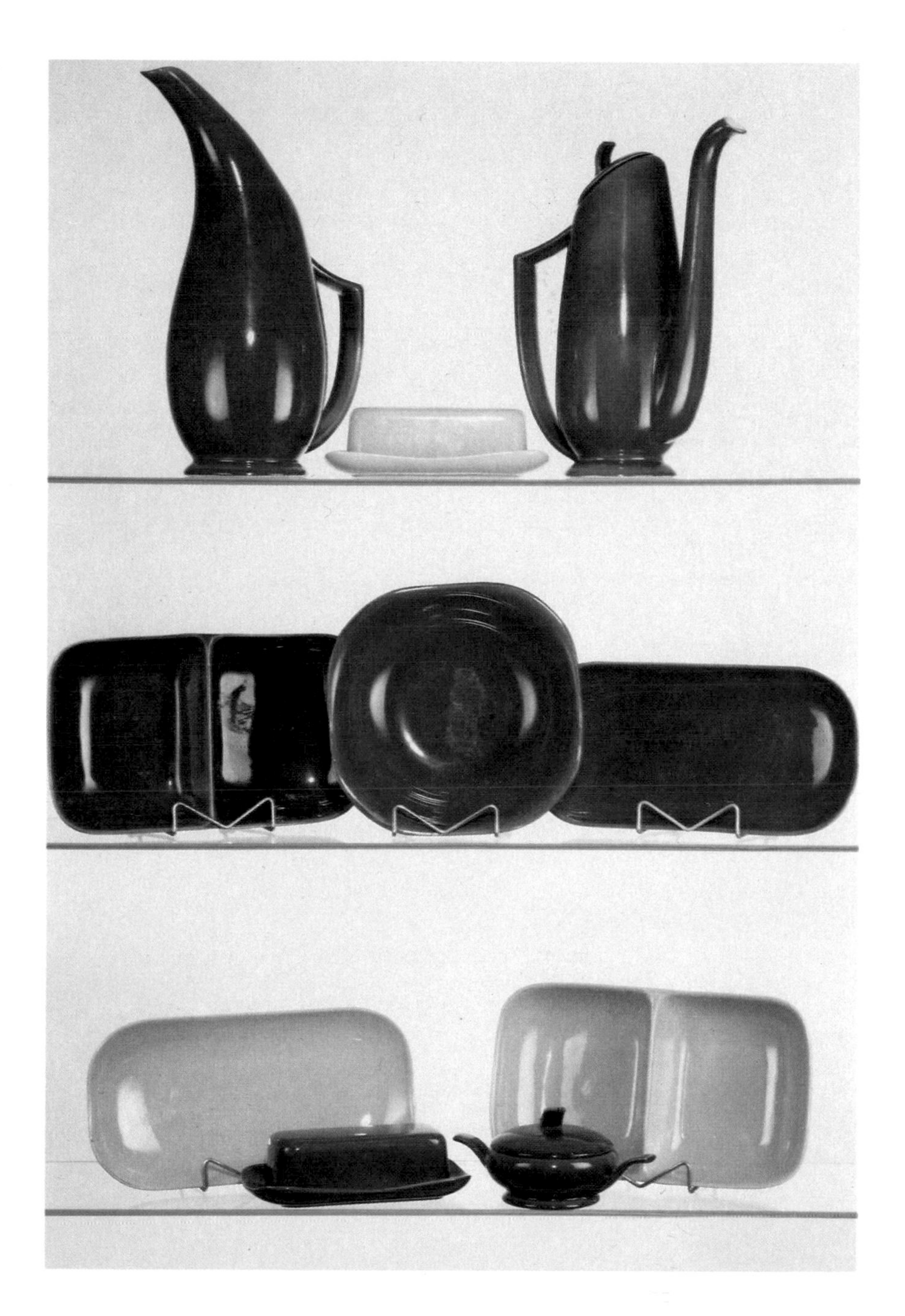

56453

Plate XXXIX

Row 1

1. Morning Glory blue 13" platter. 2. Morning Glory blue dessert bowl. 3. Morning Glory blue vegetable bowl.
Current Value: 1. $8.00; 2. $4.00; 3. $7.00.

Row 2

1. Montmarte French sidewalk cafe scene futura shape dinner plate. 2. Montmarte bread & butter plate. 3. Montmarte cup & saucer set. 4. Montmarte divided relish dish.
Current Value: 1. $5.00; 2. $4.00; 3. $9.00; 4. $9.00.

Row 3

1. Morning Glory pink dinner plate. 2. Morning Glory pink cup & saucer set. 3. Morning Glory pink dessert dish. 4. Morning Glory pink vegetable dish.
Current Value: 1. $5.00; 2. $8.00; 3. $5.00; 4. $7.00.

Plate XXXX

Row 1

1. Lexington dinner plate, concord shape. 2. Lexington cream pitcher. 3. Lexington covered sugar bowl. 4. Lexington teapot. 5. Lexington coffee cup. 6. Lexington bread & butter plate.
Current Value: 1. $5.00; 2. $6.00; 3. $6.00; 4. $15.00; 5. $5.00; 6. $5.00.

Row 2

1. Orleans dinner plate provincial shape. 2. Orleans tea-pot. 3. Orleans sugar bowl. 4. Orleans dinner plate.
Current Value: 1. $6.00; 2. $15.00; 3. $7.00; 4. $6.00.

Row 3

1. Two Step dinner plate. 2. Two Step salt & pepper shakers. 3. Two Step sugar & creamer set. 4. Two Step bread & butter plate. 5. Two Step saucer.
Current Value: 1. $5.00; 2. $7.00; 3. $15.00 set; 4. $4.00; 5. $4.00.

Plate XXXXI

Row 1

1. Kashmir bread & butter plate. 2. Random Harvest dinner plate.
Current Value: 1. $6.00; 2. $5.00.

Row 2

1. Hotel or Restaurant china oval bakers bowl. 2. Driftwood anniversary shape dinner plate. 3. Orleans salad plate.
Current Value: 1. $4.00; 2. $8.00; 3. $5.00.

Row 3

1. Hotel china white glazed plate. 2. Hotel china 10" platter white glaze. 3. Hotel china speckled tea-pot.
Current Value: 1. $4.00; 2. $5.00; 3. $6.00.

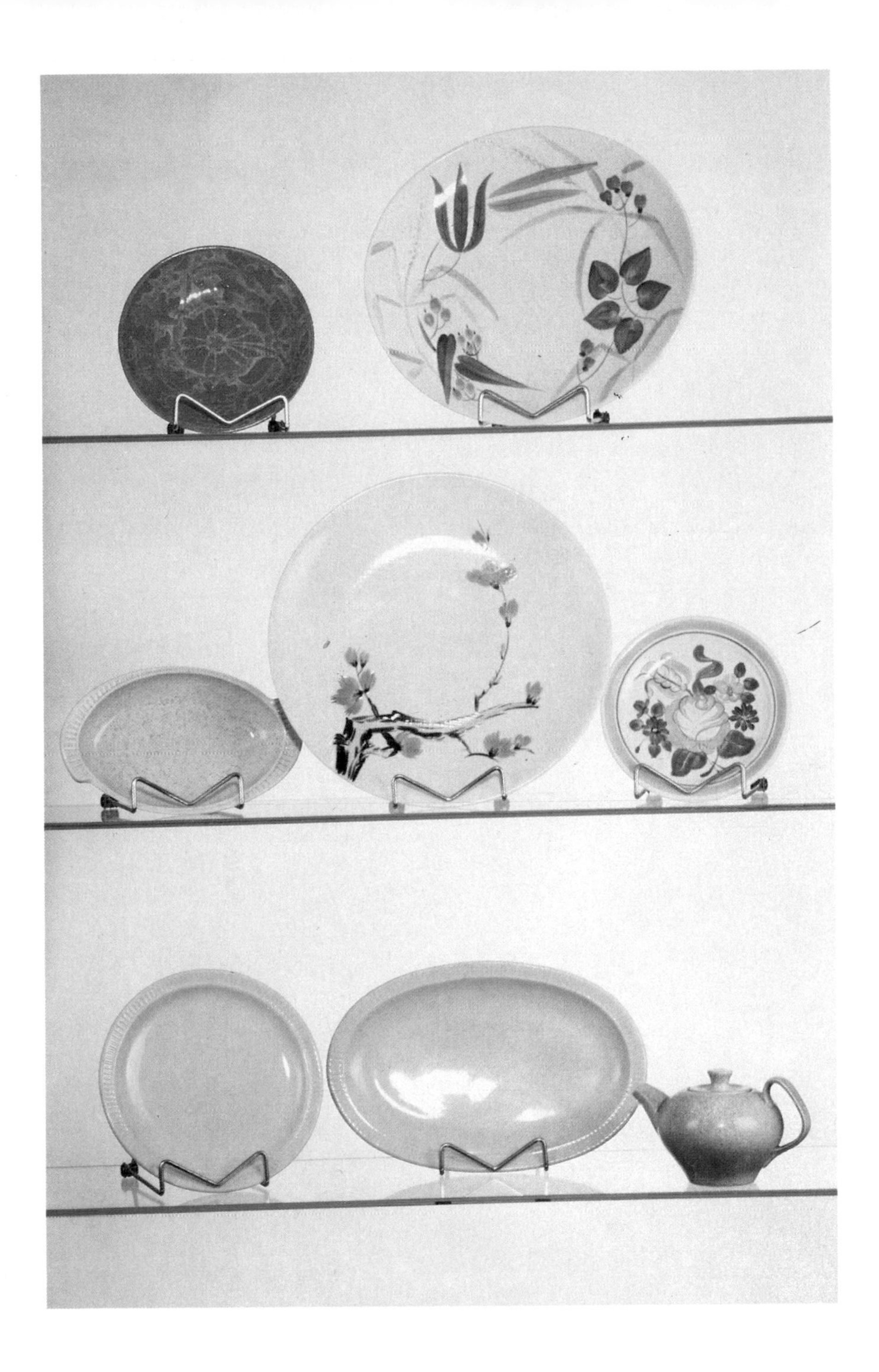

Plate XXXXII

Row 1

1. Pink Spice cream pitcher. 2. Grey Spice tall pitcher. 3. Grey spice cream pitcher.
Current Value: 1. $7.00; 2. $10.00; 3. $7.00.

Row 2

1. Grey Spice tall salt & pepper shaker. 2. Grey Spice small salt & pepper shakers. 3. Green Spice butter dish anniversary shape. 4. Green Spice cream pitcher. 5. Grey Spice sugar bowl.
Current Value: 1. $4.00; 2. $6.00; 3. $12.00; 4. $6.00; 5. $6.00.

Row 3

1. Ebb Tide salad plate. 2. Ebb Tide dinner plate. 3. Ebb Tide bread & butter plate.
Current Value: 1. $4.00; 2. $5.00; 3. $4.00.

Plate XXXXIII
Stoneware

Row 1

1. Planter, grey & tan, green glazed interior, figures of trees, sky, water, castle and grass, no mark. 2. Flower pot, marked with stamped blue circle Red Wing Union Stoneware Company Red Wing Minnesota. 3. Bowl, green & brown, marked with stamped blue circle Red Wing Union Stoneware Company Red Wing Minnesota.
Current Value: 1. $18.00; 2. $12.00; 3. $15.00.

Row 2

1. Vase, floral and leaf decor, marked with stamped blue circle Red Wing Union Stoneware Company Red Wing Minnesota. 2. Vase, grey & tan, figures of flamingo birds, cattails and plants, no marks.
Current Value: 1. $25.00; 2. $22.00.

Row 3

1. Bean pot, Provincial dinner and bakeware, three quart size. 2. Casserole, Provincial dinner and bakeware, three quart size. 3. Marmite, Provincial dinner and bakeware, twelve oz. size. 4. Casserole, Provincial dinner and bakeware, 1½ quart size.
Current Value: 1. $6.00; 2. $7.00; 3. $5.00; 4. $5.00.

The Provincial dinner and bakeware is a modern set manufactured by the Red Wing Pottery Company. The colors were a natural beige with cover accents of brilliant bittersweet. The dinnerware was oven proof and detegent safe. The set consisted of plates 6" and 10" in size, cereal bowl, platter, coffee cup & saucer, large and small oval dish, salt & pepper shakers, beverage mug, syrup jug, water pitcher, sugar, cream pitcher, egg dish, butter dish and vegetable bowl along with the above pictured items. A service for 8 originally sold for $16.95.

Plate XXXXIV

Row 1

1. Bowl, spongeware, marked with blue stamp Red Wing Oven Ware. 2. Jar, stoneware, raised mark Minnesota Stoneware Company Red Wing Minnesota.
Current Value: 1. $35.00; 2. $22.00.

Row 2

1. Jug, stoneware, raised mark Minnesota Stoneware Company Red Wing Minnesota. 2. Bird feeder, marked on front - Stoneware Red Wing Ko-Rec Feeder patent #1, 783, 780. Made only by the Red Wing Potteries Inc. Red Wing Minnesota. Set on a level.
Current Value: 1. $22.00; 2. $35.00.

Row 3

1. Top-crock, stoneware two gallon size, marked on front with a stamped wing in red, also blue stamped mark in circle Red Wing Stoneware Company Red Wing Minnesota. 2. Bottom left - crock, stoneware two gallon size, marked on front with two stamped leaves in blue, also blue stamped mark in circle Red Wing Union Stoneware Company Red Wing Minnesota. 3. Bottom right - crock, stoneware stamped mark in circle Red Wing Union Stoneware Company Red Wing Minnesota, stamped with 2 blue leaves.
Current Value: 1. $25.00; 2. $25.00; 3. $25.00.

REC FEEDER
PATENT No. 1,763,780
MADE ONLY BY
RED WING POTTER
ED WING, - MIN
ET ON A LEVE
RED WING
UNION STONEWARE
CO
UNION
STONEWARE CO.

Rum Rill Art Pottery

Red Wing Potteries produced art pottery for the Rum Rill Pottery Company in the early 1930's. The pottery pieces were marked Rum Rill and distributed around the country by a local jobber. The Red Wing Company used several of their own molds to manufacture pieces of pottery for Rum Rill. This applied to the swans, cornucopias, vases and other pieces. Often one finds duplicate pieces, both marked differently.

Plate XXXXV

Row 1

1. Vase, semi-gloss blue, impressed mark Rum Rill #320. 2. Planter, matte white, impressed mark Rum Rill #304. 3. Planter, matte pink, hat shape, impressed mark Rum Rill #H-36 U.S.A. 4. Bowl, matte green, pumpkin shape, impressed mark Rum Rill #267.
Current Value: 1. $12.00; 2. $12.00; 3. $10.00; 4. $9.00.

Row 2

1. Vase, semi-gloss blue, fanned with handles, impressed mark Rum Rill #272. 2. Vase, matte pink, scallop decor, impressed mark Rum Rill #H32-U.S.A. 3. Planter, semi-gloss ivory, low leaf decor, impressed mark Rum Rill #F-40. 4. Planter, matte blue spatter, impressed mark Rum Rill #315.
Current Value: 1. $12.00; 2. $12.00; 3. $6.00; 4. $8.00.

Row 3

1. Planter, matte white, impressed mark Rum Rill #E-12. 2. Vase, matte orange to green, impressed mark Rum Rill #290. 3. Vase, matte orange to lavender, impressed mark Rum Rill #427. 4. Ashtray, matte green with brown, impressed mark Rum Rill #E-15.
Current Value: 1. $8.00; 2. $14.00; 3. $15.00; 4. $6.00.

Row 4

1. Planter, matte pink, impressed mark Rum Rill U.S.A. 2. Vase, matte pink, impressed mark Rum Rill #J-17 U.S.A. 3. Basket, semi-gloss white, impressed mark Rum Rill #285. 4. Book-ends, fan & scroll design, has gold wing sticker saying "Rum Rill", also impressed mark #391.
Current Value: 1. $8.00; 2. $8.00; 3. $15.00; 4. $15.00 pr.

Plate XXXXVI

Row 1

1. Vase, matte white, marked with blue and silver Rum Rill U.S.A. sticker. 2. Vase, semi-gloss white to brown, impressed mark Rum Rill #514. 3. Planter, matte yellow, impressed mark Rum Rill #498.
Current Value: 1. $6.00; 2. $12.00; 3. $12.00.

Row 2

1. Vase, matte white, hanging Deco style, impressed mark Rum Rill #600-6". 2. Vase, matte green, impressed mark Rum Rill #636. 3. Vase, matte white, hanging swirl design, impressed mark Rum Rill #601.
Current Value: 1. $14.00; 2. $10.00; 3. $14.00.

Row 3

1. Bud Vase, matte green, impressed mark Rum Rill #329. 2. Vase, matte pink, impressed mark Rum Rill. 3. Vase, semi-gloss white, impressed mark Rum Rill #H7-U.S.A. 4. Planter, matte white, impressed mark Rum Rill #273.
Current Value: 1. $10.00; 2. $8.00; 3. $8.00; 4. $8.00.

Row 4

1. Planter, semi-gloss blue, impressed mark Rum Rill #436. 2. Vase, matte turquoise, deco style, impressed mark Rum Rill #569. 3. Planter, semi-gloss white, impressed mark Rum Rill #623.
Current Value: 1. $15.00; 2. $35.00; 3. $8.00.

Plate XXXXVII

Row 1

1. Vase, matte turquoise to brown, impressed mark Rum Rill #630. 2. Vase, semi-gloss white, impressed mark Rum Rill U.S.A. 3. Planter, matte orange to green, impressed mark Rum Rill #277. 4. Vase, matte ivory, impressed mark Rum Rill U.S.A.
Current Value: 1. $10.00; 2. $10.00; 3. $14.00; 4. $8.00.

Row 2

1. Vase, matte green, impressed mark Rum Rill #10. 2. Vase, matte brown to orange, impressed mark Rum Rill #668. 3. Vase, matte peach, impressed mark Rum Rill #H-10.
Current Value: 1. $12.00; 2. $12.00; 3. $12.00.

Row 3

1. Vase, matte turquoise, impressed mark Rum Rill #13. 2. Vase, matte turquoise, swirl decor, impressed mark Rum Rill #I-24. 3. Vase, matte blue, impressed mark Rum Rill #308.
Current Value: 1. $15.00; 2. $18.00; 3. $15.00.

Row 4

1. Vase, matte blue, impressed mark Rum Rill #47. 2. Vase, matte blue, impressed mark Rum Rill #308. 3. Vase, matte blue, impressed mark Rum Rill #303. 4. Vase, matte blue, impressed mark Rum Rill #506.
Current Value: 1. $15.00; 2. $15.00; 3. $8.00; 4. $8.00.

The following Red Wing dinnerware sets are factory brochures that show some of the dinner lines that are not pictured in this book: Hearthstone Orange, Hearthstone Beige, Kashmir, Pepe, Brocade, Blue Shadows, and Damask.

HEARTHSTONE BEIGE
by Red Wing
Sears
Available at Sears Retail Stores Only

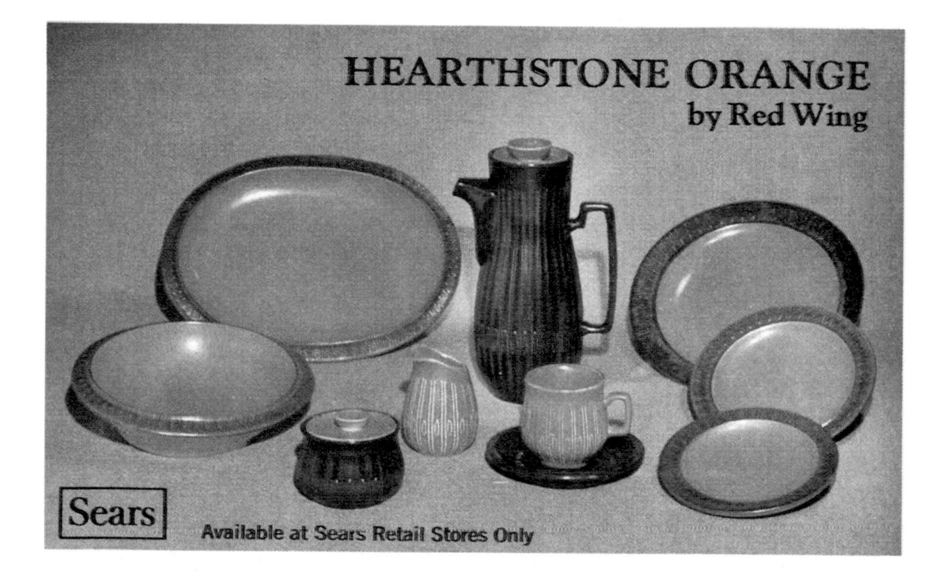
HEARTHSTONE ORANGE
by Red Wing
Sears
Available at Sears Retail Stores Only

Blue Shadows
by Red Wing

Brocade
by Red Wing

Kashmir
RED WING POTTERIES, Inc.
RED WING, MINNESOTA
Damask
RED WING POTTERIES, Inc.
RED WING, MINNESOTA